AUSTIN VAL VERDE

A Montecito Masterpiece

AUSTIN VAL VERDE

A MONTECITO MASTERPIECE

Photographs by Berge Aran

Introduction by Berge Aran and Gail Jansen

Austin Val Verde Foundation | Santa Barbara, California

To the memory of Dr. and Mrs. Warren R. Austin

Printed in South Korea

PUBLISHED BY the Austin Val Verde Foundation
            P.O. Box 5519
            Santa Barbara, CA 93150

DISTRIBUTED BY Balcony Press
            512 East Wilson Avenue, Suite 213
            Glendale, CA 91206

EDITOR Jay Belloli
TEXT EDITOR Karen Jacobson
DESIGNER Leslie Baker Graphic Design
PRINTER Navigator Cross-media

ISBN 1-890449-39-3

Library of Congress Control Number: 2005934203

COVER Pond looking toward the Main House

CONTENTS

FOREWORD

t is my joy to make available the first comprehensive photographic essay on a place that has played a significant, if little-known, role in America's cultural landscape. At first, you may flip through the pages thinking, "Oh, I've seen this before," but I assure you that you have not. Even though Austin Val Verde has been the photographic subject of hundreds of garden books and articles since its inception in 1896, it has never been fully documented in a monograph of its own. Its story is worth telling and worth reading about.

I fell in love with Val Verde the moment I first drove into this magical place, deep in the woods under a canopy of trees that create intimate spaces of astonishing beauty. Its owners, Dr. and Mrs. Warren R. Austin, had the habit of saying little about "the place" because their delight was in watching their guests' enthusiasm grow as they began to "see" what the Austins already knew existed. That was in the late 1980s. I sought their permission to begin researching the estate and its stories for an academic book on its history. They were happy to have finally found someone who would dedicate the effort and were generous in their support of the project.

By the time I met Berge Aran in 1993, I was working on my graduate degree in architecture at the University of California, Los Angeles. For many years Berge was a lecturer in architectural history and curator of the audiovisual collection for the UCLA School of Architecture. His position represented part of the classical structure of the American architectural curriculum within a university, so he was well regarded and much depended upon.

But I saw something else about Berge. When I sat in his classes, he spoke with an authentic voice about the ancient cultures that came from the deserts of the Middle East. He posed questions concerning the value of light and shadow in an architectural space created by the desert. He sought explanations of walls that were the windblown faces of cliffs. As I listened to him, I began to recognize my own inadequacies in telling the whole story of Val Verde. Bertram Goodhue, Val Verde's famous architect, had also lain in Berge's deserts and pondered Berge's questions. Berge was Turkish born; was educated at the University of Rome, in the shadow of the Vatican; and had finally settled in the United States.

Berge and I became research partners on the Val Verde project for three years, until his death in 2000. During that time he was given access to photograph Val Verde, which is what he wanted to do the most. We scribbled notes to each other about our latest clues or caught each other between classes for a sentence or two, but his real research was the photography.

Berge; his wife, Barbara; and their young daughter, Anna, would arrive for the weekend with cameras, tripods, lenses, and film. Each photograph was an experiment designed to highlight some hidden aspect of the place that Berge had noticed. Few details escaped his attention. Very little was denied his camera's eye. The photographs began to pour out, telling their own story.

These photographs are a privileged view captured by a man whose life was dedicated to gleaning the most perfect images of the world's architecture. But they also reveal Berge. They explain the man who always stood behind the camera because they show us what moved him to create. He had an eye for beauty and a passion for the light that played over this California landscape. Berge demanded authenticity personally and in everything he touched as a teacher or a student. He was a perfect gentleman of the Old World, schooled in the arts of humility and service. Where a less cultured man may have seen a cluttered, overgrown environment, Berge saw the source materials of great opera sets inhabited by heroic characters. He; Dr. Austin; and Leland Jansen, the Austin's friend and trustee, delighted in this conversation as much as Wright Ludington and his guests had years before.

Austin Val Verde colonnade

This photographic essay is the first comprehensive work to be published on the subject of Austin Val Verde. Others will follow with written commentary, different interpretive images, and varying points of view. Berge Aran's contribution sets a high standard that we will strive to equal in these future publications.

Gail Jansen
Executive Director–President
Austin Val Verde Foundation

INTRODUCTION

BASED ON TEXTS BY BERGE ARAN AND GAIL JANSEN

ustin Val Verde is an almost enchanted place in Montecito, California, and one of the greatest of the Southern California garden estates. It contains a landmark house by one of the most significant American architects of the early twentieth century and more than seventeen acres of world-famous gardens. Val Verde is an international attraction for architects, landscape architects, garden designers, and historians of American culture in part because, in contrast to those of so many estates of the period, its house and gardens still reveal much of its early history. Part of its magic stems from the presence of notable artists and intellectuals at the estate from the 1920s through the 1990s. Film legends like Gloria Swanson, Tallulah Bankhead, Katharine Hepburn, and Vincent Price were also frequent houseguests.

The architecture and original garden layout of Val Verde were designed by Bertram Grosvenor Goodhue (1869–1924), who was celebrated during his lifetime as the leading American church architect in the American Gothic Revival style and as one of the individuals who paved the way for American modernism. Goodhue started his mature career in Boston as a partner of Ralph Adams Cram, the other important American Gothic Revival ecclesiastical architect of the period. Around 1914 Goodhue established his own practice in New York. His acknowledged masterpieces are the Nebraska State Capitol in Lincoln (1923–25), the Los Angeles Central Library (1922–24), and his overall design of the Panama-Pacific Exposition in Balboa Park, San Diego (1915). Goodhue designed Val Verde while he was the supervising architect of the exposition.

The austere residence of Val Verde stands as a major turning point in Goodhue's career and in American architecture. It is the first mature residence in the Mexican Spanish Colonial Revival architectural style, which Goodhue originated in the United States. But in Val Verde's mansion Goodhue transcended his sixteenth-century sources and created a home that, with its simple lines, anticipates American modernism. Goodhue's new architectural style inspired the proliferation of the Spanish Colonial Revival style in Southern California in the 1910s and 1920s through the work of his protégés Elmer Grey, Myron Hunt, Reginald Johnson, George Washington Smith, and Carleton Winslow. Such an extensive architectural project as the "New Spain" of Santa Barbara, created after a devastating earthquake in 1925, exemplifies the later development of this style. Because of the proximity in time to the Spanish American War of 1898, however, the name of this innovative style was quickly changed to the Mediterranean and then the California style. Goodhue received numerous commissions from Southern California clients for projects in this style, including the Montecito Country Club, the California Institute of Technology campus, Los Angeles Central Library, and the 150-acre Naval Training

Bertram Goodhue, "El Fureidis," 1902–24, built for James Waldron Gillespie, showing the flight of stairs connecting the house to the Persian-inspired gardens.

Center in San Diego. After decades of relative neglect, there has been a great increase in interest in Goodhue's architecture in the last twenty-five years as a result of the rise of postmodern architecture, an approach that integrates modernism with historical influences. Goodhue's imaginative exploration of historical architecture and his creation of a modern architecture with historical references have been seen as relevant to the eclecticism of postmodernism.

Goodhue was commissioned to build Val Verde as a summer home for New York coffee trader Henry Dater. The Dater estate, or Dias Felices, as it was originally named, was an extension of Goodhue's design for the contiguous and extensive Persian-inspired estate El Fureidis, created earlier for James Waldron Gillespie, Dater's first cousin and Goodhue's lifelong friend. Val Verde was conceived and built in stages throughout much of Goodhue's career. But the fixed architecture of the main house and grounds was built between 1915 and 1919. Goodhue continued to work on details of the design until his death. Since Dater and his family rarely stayed at Val Verde, it became Goodhue's personal retreat for much of the time, a site that, along with its neighboring estate, was clearly close to his heart.

When Goodhue died suddenly in 1924, Dater sold the estate to Charles Ludington, the editor-in-chief of the *Saturday Evening Post* and the founder of an East Coast commuter airline that later became American Airlines. When Ludington died in 1927, he willed the property to one of his sons, Wright. Before his father purchased Val Verde, Wright Ludington and his friend Lockwood de Forest Jr. (1896–1949), an aspiring landscape architect, made a trip to visit all of Goodhue's buildings. Clearly, when he told his father that he wanted Val Verde as his inheritance, Wright Ludington already had a plan for the estate in mind. This is astonishing, considering that he was still in his twenties. He engaged de Forest to help him transform Goodhue's Mexican Spanish Colonial Revival estate into a classical villa filled with Hellenistic and Roman sculpture—a suitable backdrop for the accomplished artists and intellectuals who made up Ludington's circle. The Val Verde commission lasted the rest of de Forest's life and became his masterpiece.

In addition to being de Forest's patron and mentor, Ludington commissioned a collection of rooms by some of the leading decorative artists of the period. Oliver Messel, set and costume designer for Covent Garden in London and for the Hollywood studios, created the exotic "Red Tent" master bedroom suite in 1939, which received rave reviews in the art journals. Noted New York Metropolitan Opera set designer Eugene Berman was selected to create a bedroom suite using the famous "Berman blue," which usually elicited bravos from sophisticated opera audiences.

For several reasons, both personal and political, by 1955 Ludington sold Val Verde. Marjorie Temple Buell owned it for several weeks and then sold it to Florence "Bunny" Heath Horton (1915–91). Bunny was an avid horsewoman and golfer who had also inherited the Chicago Bridge and Iron Company, the largest engineering firm in the world at that time. She purchased Val Verde as a wedding present for her fiancé, Dr. Warren R. Austin (1911–99).

Dr. Austin had arrived in Santa Barbara after World War II with a handwritten letter of introduction from the duke and duchess of Windsor to a network of local Anglophiles and English expatriates. During the war Dr. Austin had been the personal physician of the duke and duchess but was primarily their bridge partner while the duke was governor of the Bahamas. When he first came to Santa Barbara, he stayed with Beryl Markham, the aviator, and soon moved to Val Verde to be Ludington's personal physician in residence. In fact, Dr. Austin became Montecito's first resident physician, soon establishing his own clinic there. Among the doctor's close friends were actress Dame Judith Anderson, whom he produced in her Tony-winning *Hamlet*; Michael Hallifax, the director of the National Repertoire Theater in London and later artistic director of the Globe Theater; and Tony Brown, who had been aide-de-camp to the duke and royal escort to the queen. He also maintained lifelong relationships with a number of doctors, whom he helped to establish themselves in Santa Barbara.

In contrast to Wright Ludington's strong desire to change the estate, Dr. and Mrs. Austin decided to implement a European style of management, focusing on conservation. They allowed the house and grounds to take on a lived-in appearance. They were assisted by their friend and trustee, Leland Jansen, and head gardeners John Cocuzza and Luis Almanza, who were of Italian and Mexican descent, respectively. The contribution of the gardeners, who subtly reshaped the grounds by reviving Italian and Spanish-Mexican themes, reasserted compositional ideas from Goodhue and de Forest.

While continuing to practice medicine, Dr. Austin pursued a theatrical career. He became an impresario, the West Coast partner of the famous New York stage producer Sol Hurok. The doctor financed and helped plan the importation of the first Broadway plays—including scenery, cast, and technical staff—to Santa Barbara and Los Angeles. He also brought the Vienna Boys Choir and the Metropolitan Opera to California, which inspired his friends to establish the Los Angeles Opera, the Music Academy of the West, Santa Barbara's Lobero Theater, and other institu-

Bertram Goodhue, Austin Val Verde ("Dias Felices"), 1915–18, shortly after it was completed. Note the original formal entrance on the right, which Lockwood de Forest Jr. redesigned.

tions that have contributed to the region's rich cultural tradition.

During both Ludington's and the Austins' ownership of Val Verde, legendary figures visited or stayed at the house. A signed photograph by Katharine Hepburn still graces a downstairs hallway, given perhaps during a visit to the estate with her friend George Cukor, the director of many of her best films, who frequented Val Verde for Sunday brunch when Los Angeles was too hot. Christopher Isherwood came as a guest after he left W. H. Auden. Charles Lindbergh and his wife stayed to escape "the public." Georgia O'Keeffe was given an "opening" by Ludington and left behind a painting that is now owned by the Santa Barbara Museum of Art. People came to "just walk" the grounds or to renew their creative energy, and many came to have fun, at afternoon gatherings with the likes of Cole Porter or Noel Coward. During Goodhue's time, and then during Ludington's and the Austins' residences at Val Verde, the estate was an important center for social and cultural exchange for members of the world's elite.

Although Dr. and Mrs. Austin owned many residences around the world, preserving Val

Verde was important to them. Dr. Austin described it this way: "I was a simple boy from a little town and a family that had very little money. The first time I arrived at Val Verde it changed my life. It gave me hope that life could be as I dreamed it could be. I wanted everyone to have that same experience, that same sense of hope." In 1994, five years before his death, Dr. Austin made legal arrangements to make the estate a foundation, thereby preserving its unique contributions to architecture, landscape design, and the history of culture in Southern California.

NAMES OF THE AUSTIN VAL VERDE ESTATE:

Dias Felices (1896–1925): *owner, Henry Dater; architect, Bertram Goodhue; landscape architect, Charles Gibbs Adams*

Val Verde (1925–55): *owner, Wright S. Ludington; designer, Lockwood de Forest Jr.*

Val Verde (1955–99): *owners, Dr. and Mrs. Warren R. Austin; manager and trustee, Lee Jansen; head gardeners, John Cocuzza and Luis Almanza*

Austin Val Verde (2000–): *owner, Austin Val Verde Foundation; executive director–president, Gail Jansen, Assoc. A.I.A.*

The experience of entering Austin Val Verde conveys both artistic intent and hospitality. This curved drive, flanked by lush vegetation, leads to the motor court, barely visible in the distance. The visitor has no visual preparation for the extraordinary Main House, which will soon come into view.

Entrance road to Austin Val Verde, designed by Bertram Goodhue with landscaping designed by Lockwood de Forest Jr.

Ceremonial procession is a central experience at Austin Val Verde. The round motor court is like a compass. To the east is the main entrance to the mansion. To the north is an archway to smaller buildings constructed to de Forest's designs. To the south is the gated entrance to the estate. To the west are an arch and an intimate walkway that leads to what used to be the estate's Tower House.

MOTOR COURT DESIGNED BY BERTRAM GOODHUE, WITH BLACK-AND-WHITE HARD SURFACE ADDED BY LOCKWOOD DE FOREST JR.

This simple, massive rampart form impressed itself on Goodhue's mind during his visits to the Spanish Colonial monuments in Mexico in the 1890s and from his experiences of Roman ruins in Spain and the "La Cabana" fortress in Havana. It finally emerged in his design for Austin Val Verde.

THE WEST FACADE, ORIGINALLY DESIGNED BY BERTRAM GOODHUE AS THE COMMER-CIAL ENTRANCE AND REDESIGNED BY LOCKWOOD DE FOREST JR. AS THE MAIN ENTRANCE

Simple, monumental, and modern in form, this American castle received royalty, celebrities, and ordinary people alike with elegance and charm.

WEST FACADE, LEFT SECTION

There is an absolute incongruity in this space. A lightless, cavelike hall is unified with an ancient panel from Pompeii, which is combined with a pair of wooden corbels and a contemporary mirror from a local store. Standing in this entryway, the visitor immediately feels the dramatic atmosphere of the Main House.

THE INTERIOR ENTRANCE, WITH WRIGHT LUDINGTON'S ENTRANCE CONSOLE

The understated simplicity of Goodhue's front hall has been transformed over time by the furniture and objects of those who have lived here.

ENTRANCE HALL FACING NORTH

This light-filled space leads, to the left, into the central atrium and, to the right, to a view over the beautiful reflecting pools and swimming pool on the south side of the mansion. The staircase and hall reveal Goodhue's instinctive sense of line, its power expressed even in three-dimensional space.

MAIN STAIRCASE AND HALL, LOOKING EAST

The discreet arched door under the staircase leads to a tiny room that was used by Dr. Austin for years as an office and as a retreat from patients, staff, guests, and family.

MAIN STAIRCASE LOOKING UP TOWARD THE SECOND FLOOR

Goodhue's oversize French doors of old glass act as a curtain between the cool, dark interior hall and the sun and warmth of the atrium.

Inspired by the traditions of Islamic architecture, Goodhue made this space the center of the Main House. The stone table, added by Lockwood de Forest Jr., serves as a pedestal for Isamu Noguchi's sculpture *Capital II*, which provides a napping space for cats or, on rainy days, a birdbath.

ATRIUM

The black-and-white awning slid on iron rings along wire strung across the patio, creating a romantic space for favored guests, while the decorative open grilles provided a glimpse of the events taking place below.

Goodhue's small but exquisite shelter protects from the sun and rain, providing a beautiful place from which to contemplate the night.

These famous blue glass tiles traveled a number of times before they were given a home here in the atrium. In the 1890s they could be seen in the Tenth Street de Forest family home, now a New York City landmark. Originally some of the tiles were part of a Middle Eastern edifice from as early as 300 C.E.

Installation of Islamic tiles by Lockwood de Forest Jr.

Sitting within the shelter of the three arches and surrounded by the antique tiles, one has a sense of having escaped to another place and time.

INSIDE THE ARCADE LOOKING OUT ON THE ATRIUM

Goodhue designed the living room as the
anteroom for the atrium, and when the doors
are flung open and the breeze rushes through,
they almost became one continuous space.
The living room faces east and fills with the
morning sun. By midmorning the light
recedes into shadows. All of Berge Aran's
indoor and outdoor photographs were taken
using existing natural illumination. He wanted
to convey, as much as possible, exactly what it
was like to be in any of the spaces on the estate.

LIVING ROOM

Dr. and Mrs. Austin loved to have their dinner by candlelight so that they could enjoy the sense of being suspended among the ancient trees, the camellias, and the fountains. Out the north window, on the left of the photograph, is a beautiful reflecting pool whose focal point is a twentieth-century sculpture of Pericles at its far end.

Dining room, with the north and east windows

Looking out from dining room onto the water terrace and exedra was the privilege of the person at the head of the dining table. It is said that—in that chair—Wright Ludington conceived of the first night lighting for landscape in America. His World War II bullet lights still cling to the olive trees and play an important part in the drama of the view.

DINING ROOM WATER TERRACE, DESIGNED BY LOCKWOOD DE FOREST JR.

This allée of concrete columns is Austin Val Verde's most famous site. It is so perfectly designed that the columns feel as if they have always been here, and one is reminded of places from the Baroque period or even from ancient Roman or Hellenistic times. They appear to have been conjured up to provide an ideal setting for Wright Ludington's magnificent collection of Greek and Roman art.

COLUMN ALLÉE, DESIGNED BY LOCKWOOD DE FOREST JR.

Facing east, the terraces extend north and south, but their central stairway is focused on the living room, and it descends in measured stages toward the monumental pond. In the morning, level by level, the sun illuminates this area, covering the hedges and columns in golden light.

GOODHUE'S POND FROM THE TERRACES, WHICH ARE A COMBINATION OF HIS DESIGN AND THAT OF DE FOREST

The columns give a sense of monumental rhythm to the east side of the estate, and visitors feel a sense of procession as they walk on the brick path between them. At times the pond mirrors the columns and terraces, doubling the experience of their majesty.

POND LOOKING NORTH TOWARD THE COLUMNS

This is the most celebrated view of Val Verde. It captures Goodhue's masterful decision to place the Main House as if on a terrace and de Forest's brilliant addition of the allée of columns. This vantage point also shows how the symmetry of the mansion's east facade is echoed by the order of the columns and the central descending stairs.

Over the years, Berge Aran took many photographs of this magnificent view from the east of the Main House, columns, and terraces. He spent long periods of time waiting for the best light on any particular day, wanting to show how the sun and weather at the estate changed through the hours and at different times of year.

POND LOOKING TOWARD MAIN HOUSE

The more than seventeen acres of the estate are a tapestry of native California oaks, many planted after James Gillespie bought the property for his cousin Henry Dater, but a number, including this one, are ancient inhabitants, their integration into the architecture testifying to Goodhue's innate sensitivity to nature.

POND LOOKING TOWARD NORTH OAK

One of the passions revealed in Berge Aran's long photographic exploration of Austin Val Verde was his desire to capture as many views of the estate as possible. This vista looks from the pond toward one of the most magnificent trees on the property and one that, even though it is not native, seems natural and inevitable in its location.

The pond at Austin Val Verde has always been left to exist in its natural state without frequent cleaning. A few large koi appear from to time from underneath the water plants.

Pond looking south toward the columns and Moreton Bay fig

The pond is one of the finest points from which to survey the areas east of the Main House. The columns measure the space in this inspiring view.

POND LOOKING SOUTH TOWARD COLUMNS

Goodhue's original balustrades unite with de Forest's later clipped hedges, their brilliant green a wonderful counterpoint to the tan color of the cast concrete.

This view looks back toward the main entrance to the living room. Over the decades the estate's famous guests would have approached from this direction. The French doors on the left open onto the east terrace.

LIVING ROOM LOOKING TOWARD THE SOUTH WATER TERRACE

De Forest's monumental columns frame a glimpse of the beautiful pool beyond, designed by Goodhue and deepened for swimming at Ludington's behest. Only Berge Aran has been able to capture the water's luminous turquoise, which is seen only at certain times.

COLUMNED TERRACE ON THE SOUTH SIDE OF THE MAIN HOUSE

This was the original entrance Goodhue conceived for the mansion, but it was transformed by de Forest with the addition of the monumental columns. Here is where original owner Henry Dater and his wife would have greeted their guests during the summers when they were in residence. Bertram Goodhue stayed here much more often, and one can imagine the friends and architectural colleagues who walked through this door.

COLUMNED TERRACE ON THE SOUTH SIDE LOOKING THROUGH THE FORMAL FRONT DOOR

This carved stone sarcophagus from about 400 B.C.E. is located just below the columned terrace on the south side of the Main House. It is one of the few pieces of sculpture from Wright Ludington's notable collection that remains on the estate. Many of the paintings and sculptures that he assembled now have a permanent home at the Santa Barbara Museum of Art.

GREEK SARCOPHAGUS

The south swimming pool and reflecting pool are among the estate's most beautiful features, visible as one ascends the main stairway and from two of the guest rooms on the second floor. Berge Aran captured the glowing light seen in this photograph only once in the years he visited Val Verde.

WATER TERRACE FROM MAIN STAIRCASE BALCONY

The south-facing columned terrace and pools are enclosed at their far end by the majestic Moreton Bay fig. There are also a number of these trees near the creek, planted by James Gillespie, the original owner of El Fureidis, the neighboring estate.

MORETON BAY FIG FROM COLUMNED TERRACE

The brilliant white lotus vase seems a revelation, rising out of the rectangular swimming pool. Originally, during Wright Ludington's residence, a Greek statue of Venus was placed where the vase is now, alluding to the goddess's birth from the sea. This is one of Berge Aran's finest images of Austin Val Verde.

LOTUS VASE AND MORETON BAY FIG

The theatrical mixture of light and shade—the colonnade in shadow, the pool in sunlight—is one of the inspired touches in Lockwood de Forest's design of the grounds at Val Verde.

There are a wealth of beautiful vistas in this enchanted precinct on the south side of the mansion.

POOL LOOKING TOWARD THE MAIN HOUSE

Bertram Goodhue often made a ritual of movement from one space to another by marking the start of that journey with an arch. The stepped low walls on either side of the brick walkway define clearly where one travels to reach the circular space that is the goal.

Two of Goodhue's most memorable details on the estate are the exterior round rooms, in the exact centers of which Wright Ludington had antiquities secured for contemplation and to denote a place of arrival.

Lockwood de Forest made the experience of approaching a round room memorable by varying the plantings that one passed on the way.

TROPICAL WALKWAY TO A ROUND ROOM

The round rooms become precincts for introspection and interconnection among people. A circular cast concrete bench lines each of the rooms. As one talks to someone across the room, the curved form of the space makes every word clear and distinct, even if one speaks softly.

FULL VIEW OF A ROUND ROOM

As visitors walk on dirt paths through the beautiful trees and plants de Forest had strewn throughout the distant parts of the grounds, they come upon accents like this to delight the eye.

BLUE AGAVES GARDEN IN THE AUSTIN VAL VERDE WOODLAND

One of the delights of Austin Val Verde is the creek that runs through the estate year-round. During rainy periods one can hear the sound of flowing water throughout the estate. Berge Aran found the most felicitous view of the stream and would have waited for the sunlight to be caught by the trees.

MISSION CREEK IN AUSTIN VAL VERDE

This monument is like a shrine that one would encounter in the countryside on a journey. Goodhue would have seen spiritual objects like this in his travels. The likeness is that of the Virgin, an appropriate sacred image for an estate inspired in part by his visits to Mexico. There are memorial plaques on this monument for Dr. Austin and his wife, Florence "Bunny" Austin.

AUSTIN VAL VERDE "MARION MONUMENT," DESIGNED BY BERTRAM GOODHUE

Berge Aran's photograph shows us the powerful, curved forms created by the large branches of a group of oaks on the estate. These magnificent trees are not far from the Visitor's Cottage.

AUSTIN VAL VERDE OAKS

Lockwood de Forest varied the trees throughout the estate, providing continuity by preserving the native oaks but juxtaposing them with examples from other countries and continents.

AUSTIN VAL VERDE WOODLAND NEAR GIANT BLUE GUM EUCALYPTUS

This modest, even rustic, wood clapboard cottage offers a profound contrast to the massive concrete permanence of the Main House. Romantically placed in the woods by Lockwood de Forest, it seems almost like something out of a fairy tale.

VISITOR'S COTTAGE

These stairs may have been designed by Bertram Goodhue. They lead to the Spanish fountain, designed by Lockwood de Forest Jr., through the dense plantings de Forest also devised.

"SPANISH STAIRS" FROM OBELISKS

This arch led to the original apartment of Dr. and Mrs. Austin's business manager and trustee, Leland Jansen. It was designed by Lockwood de Forest as part of an extensive addition to Goodhue's original Main House. Details like this arch sensitively unified de Forest's new building with the original mansion.

"LEE'S LAIR" ARCHWAY

Part of de Forest's addition became an elegant retreat for "Bunny" Austin. Here, in an intimate setting, she could entertain her women friends during the day.

"Bunny's Warren" reception room

One of the major changes Wright Ludington had Lockwood de Forest make to Austin Val Verde was to transform what had been a garage area into a beautiful focus for the north arch to the motor court. A slightly raised plaza can be seen as a visitor leaves the motor court, and this Spanish fountain, designed by de Forest, was placed in its center. The fountain may have been inspired by his memories of the fountains he saw during his trip to Spain in the mid-1920s, after he and Ludington together explored the architecture, gardens, and art of Italy.

SPANISH FOUNTAIN

With his addition defining the Spanish fountain plaza on the west, Lockwood de Forest designed a wall to draw the boundary on the east. The wall was made—in color and surface—to look as ancient as the sculptures from Ludington's collection that were displayed throughout the gardens. Even the portal in the wall was oddly shaped to evoke the passage of time, as if Austin Val Verde had been present almost since the beginnings of human history.

SPANISH FOUNTAIN PLAZA WITH DE FOREST WALL

One of de Forest's most imaginative details was a curved
notch at the top of the wall to accommodate the branch
of a venerable oak tree. The branch is gone, but its shape
is poignantly still reflected in the wall.

SPANISH FOUNTAIN OAK AND WALL

As one walks through a portal to the east of the Spanish fountain plaza, one comes upon a curved wall designed by de Forest. Antiquities from Wright Ludington's collection embedded in the surface of the wall add a theatrical touch, conveying a sense that the wall has existed for centuries.

CURVED WALKWAY WITH ANTIQUITIES

As one returns from the wall of antiquities, the view of the Spanish fountain is framed in the portal, giving a sense of intimacy and drama.

WALL LOOKING BACK TOWARD THE
SPANISH FOUNTAIN

In 1939 Wright Ludington commissioned his friend Oliver Messel, a set designer from England, to transform his bathroom into a unique setting where the rituals of cleansing the body could be made theatrical. Messel created sets for the Covent Garden opera in London as well as for films during Hollywood's Golden Age. His designs for the room are not just flat murals, but are three-dimensional, creating a bathing experience unlike any other.

MASTER BATH WITH OLIVER MESSEL'S "RED TENT"

This is a view of Oliver Messel's extraordinary murals from the opposite side of the room. The door into the master bedroom can be seen on the far right

MESSEL'S DESIGN FOR THE MASTER BATH

Another view of Messel's flight of fancy for Wright Ludington's master bath.

Master bath

The "Red Tent" over the bathtub, one of the focal points of Messel's extraordinary design for Ludington's bathroom, is seen in this photograph. As always, Berge Aran photographed all of these images without artificial illumination, giving a sense of the fanciful space and dramatic light.

A DETAIL OF MESSEL'S MURALS FOR THE MASTER BATH

As noted previously, the motor court is laid out like a compass, and the arch to the west leads to a path that ends at what used to be the Tower House of the estate.

This small pond is between one of the round outdoor rooms and the building that used to be the Tower House. The thin concrete channel—in the center of the far side of the pond—formerly brought water from the Tower House, which included a water tower. From the pond the water then flowed down to the creek. The antiquity seen in this photograph has now been moved to an interior location.

<small>Austin Val Verde still pond, rocks, and antiquity</small>

This remarkable building was designed by Bertram Goodhue around 1910, remodeled by Lockwood de Forest around 1935, and reworked again by Lutah Riggs, a noted Santa Barbara architect, around 1948. It served the practical purpose of housing Henry Dater and his family while the mansion was being designed and built. But the logic of this need is belied by the design itself. It resembles a small castle out of a fairy tale, echoing the imaginary European towns that Goodhue sketched earlier in his career. Like all enchantments, the Tower House has disappeared. Now integrated into a new Montecito mansion, it has not been part of the estate for decades.

TOWER HOUSE

Also designed by Goodhue, this delicate fountain is connected by a thin, linear water channel to a small pool farther east on the estate. The fountain originally contained several objects from Wright Ludington's impressive collection of antiquities. Besides being a family residence, the Tower House also included the main source of water for the entire estate.

Tower House runlet fountain

At Ludington's directive, Lockwood de Forest transformed the Tower House atrium into a re-creation of a Roman courtyard, providing an appropriate setting for the Hellenistic and Roman sculptures from Ludington's collection that would have been displayed there.

TOWER HOUSE ATRIUM INTERIOR

BERGE ARAN

erge Aran was born in Istanbul, Turkey. He studied at the Lycée Saint-Joseph des Frères in Istanbul, an institution operated by the Jesuits. He received a degree in architecture and a Ph.D. in the history of architecture from the Department of Architecture at Istanbul Technical University and a certificate of restoration from the University of Rome, School of Architecture. He became an assistant professor at Istanbul Technical University and taught architectural history and practice. He was also the architect of excavation at a number of archaeological sites in Turkey. In Istanbul he married an American, Andrea Pfeiffenberger, who had assisted at some of these sites. While in Turkey they had a daughter, Sabina.

From early in Aran's career he was a serious photographer who documented in black-and-white a number of historic buildings in Istanbul (including structures that he helped excavate in that city) as well as buildings and archaeological sites in other parts of Turkey. The Getty Research Institute in Los Angeles has indexed many of his photographs of Turkish classical and vernacular architecture. When he moved to Los Angeles in 1972, he continued his work in photography. He and Andrea went their separate ways, but he stayed close to their daughter and often photographed her as she grew.

In 1973, appropriately, Aran became the curator of the audiovisual collection in the School of Art and Architecture at the University of California, Los Angeles, as well as a lecturer in architectural history with an emphasis on the medieval period. He was energized by teaching and by his students, and he took them several times to see pre-Columbian, Spanish Colonial, and contemporary architecture in Mexico. His photographic documentation of these trips and of sites in Southern California was extensive. In addition to his in-depth background in the ancient world, he was also knowledgeable about the contemporary arts. He published a book on Roman architecture in Asia Minor and various articles on medieval and modern architecture.

In 1983 Aran married Barbara Bennett, and they had a daughter, Anna. They frequently accompanied him when he photographed architecture in Southern California, particularly on his trips to document the architecture and gardens at Val Verde. The broad issues of culture—as well as psychology, languages, and mathematics—occupied Aran throughout his life, and he enjoyed learning new subjects. He knew Turkish, English, French, Italian, Latin, ancient Greek, and German and was learning Spanish. He was passionate and knowledgeable about music, including opera. He had been a serious violinist and violist when he was young, before he focused on architecture. He was also an avid soccer fan.

Berge Aran with his cameras at Austin Val Verde (photo: Barbara Aran)

In addition to his intellectual interests, Aran was devoted to his family, sharing with his wife, daughters, and others close to him his enthusiastic engagement with life as well as his wonderful and creative cooking. After a long illness Aran died in November 2000, close to his wife and daughters.

SELECTED BIBLIOGRAPHY

Baxter, Sylvester, Bertram Goodhue, and Henry Peabody. *Spanish Colonial Architecture in Mexico.* 10 vols. Boston: J. B. Millet Co., 1901.

Birnbaum, Charles, and Robin Karson. *Pioneers of American Landscape Design.* New York: McGraw-Hill, 2000.

Cram, Ralph Adams. *Impressions of Japanese Architecture and the Allied Arts.* London: John Lane, 1906.

De Forest, Lockwood, Sr. *Illustrations of Design; Based on Notes of Line as Used by the Craftsmen in India.* Boston: Ginn and Co., 1912.

French, Jere Stuart. *The California Garden and the Landscape Architects Who Shaped It.* Washington, D.C.: Landscape Architecture Foundation, 1993.

Garnett, Porter. *Stately Homes of California.* Boston: Little, Brown, and Co., 1915.

Gebhard, David. "The Spanish Colonial Revival in Southern California (1895–1930)." *Journal of the Society of Architectural Historians* 26 (May 1967): 131–47.

Goodhue, Bertram. *Mexican Memories: The Record of a Slight Sojourn below the Yellow Rio Grande.* New York: George M. Allen Co., 1892.

———. "Of Persian Gardens." *Century Magazine* 73 (March 1907).

———. "The Romanticist Point of View." *Craftsman* 8 (June 1905): 332–33.

Goodhue, Bertram, and Carleton Monroe Winslow. *The Architecture and Gardens of the San Diego Exposition.* San Francisco: Paul Elder and Co., 1916.

Jansen, Gail. Interviews with Kellam de Forest (b. 1926), son of Elizabeth and Lockwood de Forest Jr., 1993–2005. Transcripts, Austin Val Verde Foundation.

Jerome, Kate. *Oriental Gardening.* New York: Pantheon Books, 1997.

Mason, Penelope. *History of Japanese Art.* Englewood Cliffs, N.J.: Prentice Hall; New York: Harry N. Abrams, 1993.

Montes, Gregory. "Balboa Park, 1909–1911: The Rise and Fall of the Olmsted Plan." *Journal of San Diego History* 28 (Winter 1982): 46–67.

Mumford, Lewis. "B. G. Goodhue: Review of *Bertram Grosvenor Goodhue, Architect and Master of Many Arts.*" *New Republic,* October 28, 1925.

Neuhaus, Eugen. *San Diego Garden Fair*. San Francisco: Paul Elder and Co., 1916.

Oliver, Richard. *Bertram Grosvenor Goodhue*. New York: Architectural History Foundation; Cambridge: MIT Press, 1983.

————, ed. The *Making of an Architect, 1881–1981: Columbia University in the City of New York*. New York: Rizzoli, 1981.

Price, C. Matlock. "The Panama-California Exposition, San Diego, California: Bertram Goodhue and the Renaissance of the Spanish Colonial Style." *Architectural Record*, March 1915.

Roth, Leland. *A Concise History of American Architecture*. New York: Harper & Row, 1979.

Shand-Tucci, Douglass. *Ralph Adams Cram: Life and Architecture*. Amherst: University of Massachusetts Press, 1995.

Starr, Kevin. *Americans and the California Dream*. Oxford: Oxford University Press, 1973.

Stewart, David B. *The Making of Modern Japanese Architecture, 1868 to the Present*. Tokyo: Kodansha International, 1987.

Streatfield, David C. *California Gardens: Creating a New Eden*. New York: Abbeville Press, 1994.

Whitaker, Charles Harris, ed. *Bertram Grosvenor Goodhue: Architect and Master of Many Arts*. 1925. Reprint, New York: Da Capo Press, 1976.

Winslow, Carleton Monroe, Jr. "The Architecture of the Panama-California Exposition, 1909–1915." M.A. thesis, University of San Diego, 1976.

ACKNOWLEDGMENTS

O n behalf of Berge Aran, I would like first and foremost to acknowledge his devoted wife, Barbara, who chauffeured him to his photo shoots at Austin Val Verde so that he could concentrate on his work. She patiently waited as he experimented with lenses and light exposures and always, even now, has deferred her own talents to his. A kiss and a hug go to Anna, his younger daughter, who watched adoringly as her father "made photographs" when other daughters would have whined to be taken to the beach. Without the love and support of these two women, Berge's photography would have been exiled to family collections and scattered to the wind.

Berge would also be quick to acknowledge the phenomenal gift of Jay Belloli's contribution as editor to the preservation of his work. Berge spoke of Jay with admiration while he was alive, and every sentence of his praise has proven true. Then Berge certainly would thank Lee Jansen for his help and hospitality in providing access to Austin Val Verde. And last but not least, he would thank the late Dr. Warren R. Austin for his willingness to share his passions and his time.

As executive director–president of the Austin Val Verde Foundation, I would like to acknowledge Barbara and Anna Aran for their friendship and dedication, Jay Belloli for his skill and patience, Leslie Baker for her design of this volume, and Karen Jacobson for serving as text editor. I would like to recognize Berge's older daughter, Sabina Aran Dinsmoor, for her interest in this project. Bertram Goodhue and Lockwood de Forest Jr. must be remembered and acknowledged for their brilliance, which continues to inspire us. A thank you goes to Kellam and Peggy de Forest, who have spent a lifetime patiently telling the latest inquirer about the de Forest legacy, while storing the precious history in every nook and cranny of their home. A sincere debt of gratitude is owed to Lee Jansen for his gentleman's commitment to the legacy of Dr. and Mrs. Austin. This project would not have been possible without any one of them.

Gail Jansen